FARMINGTON COMMUNITY LIBRARY
FARMINGTON BRANCH LIBRARY
23500 LIBERTY STREET
FARMINGTON, MI 48335-3570
(248) 553-0321

JUL 1 9 2021

12 IMPOSSIBLE
DAREDEVIL STUNTS

by Samantha S. Bell

STORY LIBRARY

MORE TO EXPLORE

www.12StoryLibrary.com

12-Story Library is an imprint of Bookstaves.

Photographs ©: Lasky Corporation/Library of Congress, cover, 1; ZUMA Press, Inc./Alamy Stock Photo, 4; Jae C. Hong/Associated Press, 5; National Air and Space and Museum/PD, 6; PD, 7; annulla/CC2.0, 8; Alan Welner/Associated Press, 9; Tinseltown/Shutterstock.com, 10; Kam & Ronson/PD, 10; PD, 11; PD, 12; M.H. Zahner/Library of Congress, 13; Luisa Conlon, 14; WARNER BROS/Ronald Grant Archive/Alamy Stock Photo, 15; PD, 16; Pictorial Press Ltd/ Alamy Stock Photo, 17; Ky Michaelson/PD; Bettmann/Getty Images, 19; John H. Thurston/ Library of Congress, 20; Library of Congress, 21; DFree/Shutterstock.com, 22; Faiz Zaki/ Shutterstock.com, 23; Debbie Lawler, 24; Debbie Lawler, 25; Almazoff/Shutterstock.com, 26; Kirsty O'Connor/Alamy Stock Photo, 27; trabantos/Shutterstock.com, 28; Harry Atwell/CC3.0, 29

ISBN
9781632357380 (hardcover)
9781632358479 (paperback)
9781645820246 (ebook)

Library of Congress Control Number: 2019938680

Printed in the United States of America
July 2019

About the Cover
Harry Houdini in a promotional poster circa 1898.

Access free, up-to-date content on this topic plus a full digital version of this book. Scan the QR code on page 31 or use your school's login at 12StoryLibrary.com.

Table of Contents

Luke Aikins: Falling Back to Earth

Luke Aikins was born in Washington State in 1973. His father and grandfather were skydivers. When he grew up, he became a skydiver, too.

On July 30, 2016, 42-year-old Aikins was ready to set a world record. He was going skydiving at 25,000 feet (7,620 m) above the earth. But instead of using a parachute, he would free-fall.

Aikins had prepared for two years for the jump. He took a GPS, a communication device, and an oxygen tank. But he did not wear a wingsuit or a parachute. He didn't have anything that could slow or stop his fall. Instead, he planned to land in a high-tech safety net.

He jumped out of the Cessna airplane and faced downward. He used the air currents around him

Luke Aikins in 2017.

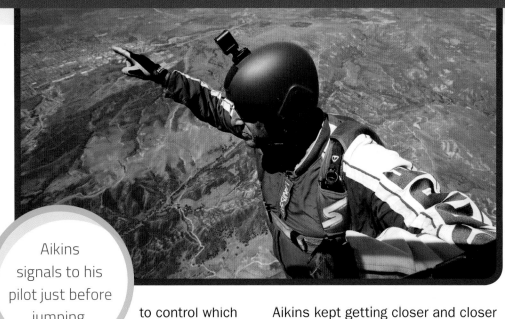

Aikins signals to his pilot just before jumping.

to control which way he went. The GPS on his helmet helped him stay in the right direction. Lights on the net turned red when he was off track. They turned white when he was on course.

Aikins kept getting closer and closer to the ground. With just one second left to go, he flipped himself over. He landed in the net on his back. The net absorbed the energy produced by his fall. The jump was successful, and Aikins walked away unharmed.

PLENTY OF PRACTICE

Aikins's family owned a skydiving business. He completed his first tandem jump when he was 12 years old. He made his first solo jump at 16. In 25 years, he completed more than 18,000 parachute jumps. Aikins works for the United States Parachute Association, where his job includes training US military special forces in skydiving.

121

Number of seconds it took for Aikins to go from the plane to the net

- The net was 100 feet long by 100 feet wide (30.5 m square).
- A news station aired Aikins's jump live.
- The stunt was called Heaven Sent.

Bessie Coleman: Daring to Fly

Bessie Coleman in 1921.

km) every day to get to school and back.

In 1915, Coleman moved to Chicago to live with her brother. She heard stories about World War I pilots. French women were flying planes. Coleman wanted to learn to fly. But because of her race, she wasn't allowed to attend a flying school in the United States. She decided to go to school in France.

Coleman taught herself French. With the help of a sponsor, she traveled to Europe in 1920. She attended France's most famous flying school. She was the only person of color in her class. In seven months, she earned her pilot's license. She came back to the United States to work as a stunt pilot. But she needed more training to do tricks. She couldn't find anyone in the United States to teach her. She went back to Europe to learn more.

Bessie Coleman was born in Texas in 1892. She was the 10th of 13 children. Her mother was African American. Her father was part African American and part Cherokee. She had to attend a segregated school. She walked four miles (6.4

34
Coleman's age when she died in an airplane accident

- She was the first African American woman awarded an international pilot's license.
- She would only perform at shows if the crowd wasn't segregated.
- Thousands of people attended her memorial service.

THINK ABOUT IT

Many people said Bessie Coleman couldn't fly. But she found a way. Can you think of a time when you had to overcome an obstacle? How did you do it?

In 1922, Coleman began traveling around the United States. She became known as Queen Bess. She did acrobatic stunts with the plane. She climbed out onto the wing and parachuted down. She died in 1926. But she overcame discrimination as an African American and as a woman.

Coleman with her plane in 1922.

Philippe Petit: Balancing Between Buildings

Philippe Petit was born in 1949 in France. As a boy, he taught himself how to walk on a rope stretched between two trees. When he was 18, he read about the World Trade Center in New York. It was still under construction. The Twin Towers had not yet been built. But Petit decided he was going to walk between them.

The stunt took six years to plan. Petit learned everything he could about the Towers. He made more than 200 visits to the building site. He took photographs, made measurements, and studied their construction. He often dressed in disguise. He pretended to be a reporter or a construction worker.

In early August 1974, Petit and his friends started stowing his equipment in the Towers. On August 6, they hid in the buildings to prepare for the event. The next morning, Petit took his position in the South Tower. He was 1,350 feet (411.5 m) above the ground with no net below.

Petit made his way back and forth across the cable eight times. He performed for

Philippe Petit in 2007.

Petit walks a tightrope suspended between the World Trade Center's Twin Towers in New York in 1974.

the crowd by sitting and even lying down on the wire. As soon as he stepped off the wire, police arrested him. But they dropped all the charges when Petit agreed to do a performance for children in Central Park.

131
Number of feet (39.9 m) between the Twin Towers

- The cable was 110 stories (363 m) high.
- Petite performed on the cable for 45 minutes.
- Petite called it "the artistic crime of the century."

PREPARING TO PERFORM

Petit taught himself other skills as well. He began learning magic tricks when he was six years old. Next, he taught himself how to juggle. He performed in the city streets for tourists. Before walking between the Towers, he walked on a wire at Notre Dame Cathedral in France and the Sydney Harbor Bridge in Australia.

Jackie Chan: Electrifying Action

Jackie Chan at a movie premier in 2017.

POLICE STORY SERIES

POLICE STORY SERIES

Jackie Chan Legendary Collection

Jackie Chan was born in Hong Kong in 1954. When he was seven years old, his parents sent him to boarding school. He studied drama, acrobatics, singing, and martial arts. After he graduated, he found a job as a stuntman. A few years later, Chan went into acting. He became known for his martial arts abilities and physical comedy. He did all of his own stunts.

Chan performed one of his most dangerous stunts for the 1985 movie *Police Story*. In the film, Chan goes after some gangsters in a shopping mall. Chan was on the top floor looking at the gangsters below.

To reach them in time, he had to jump onto a pole and slide down.

The crew wrapped the pole in Christmas lights. The lights were supposed to be plugged into a car battery. But it wasn't strong enough to light up all of them. Instead, the film crew had to plug them into the wall. Now the lights had a stronger electric current going through them. Chan was worried he might get shocked.

But the cameras started rolling. Chan leapt from a railing into the air. He grabbed the pole. The lights cracked and popped as he slid down. He

100
Distance in feet (30.5 m) Chan slid down the pole

- There was no safe landing gear.
- Instead, the crew used a prop car filled with candy.
- The crew had enough film for one take.

went through electrical sparks and shattering glass. Then he broke through a glass partition. Chan made it to the bottom. He did not get shocked, but he had second-degree burns on his hands.

Chan performing his dangerous mall stunt.

11

Annie Edson Taylor: Over the Falls

Annie Edson Taylor was born in 1839 in New York. She lived a comfortable life growing up. She married when she was 17. But her husband died in 1864 in the American Civil War. Taylor slowly ran out of money. She needed a way to earn more. In 1901, she decided she would be the first person to go over Niagara Falls in a barrel. She would either become rich and famous or die trying.

Taylor planned to go over the falls on her birthday. On October 24, 1901,

SPECIAL ORDER

Annie Taylor designed the barrel. Then she had it specially made. The inside was cushioned. There were straps inside for her to hold onto. A weight at the bottom of the barrel helped keep that end down. The other end contained an air valve that opened and closed.

Taylor and her barrel in 1901.

Niagara. Mrs. Taylor the first human being to go over Falls and lives

she climbed into the barrel and secured the lid. A boat pulled her out about a mile and a half above the falls. The barrel was cut loose and started bobbing around in the rapids.

Strong currents pulled the barrel along. It tumbled over the edge and fell with the waterfall. The barrel stayed in one piece. But the spectators weren't sure if Annie was still alive. They opened the barrel, and she was all right. The whole trip lasted about 18 minutes.

Annie tried selling postcards of herself. She wanted to go on tour and get paid to tell people what she had done. But she never made much money from her daring feat.

63
Annie Taylor's age when she went over Niagara Falls

- Frank M. Russell, a local promoter, publicized the event.
- A few days before Taylor's stunt, she and Russell tried it with her cat in the barrel.
- The cat made it safely over the falls.

Willie Harris: Breaking Barriers

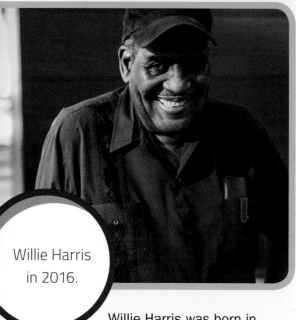

Willie Harris in 2016.

Willie Harris was born in 1941 in Mississippi. At the time, African Americans didn't have the same rights as white Americans. After serving in the US Air Force, Harris moved to Southern California. He thought things might be different there. But he faced many of the same challenges.

Harris started working as an extra in Hollywood. He wanted to a stuntman. But for many years, only white people could do stunt work. When a studio needed a stuntman with black skin, they would "paint down" a white person with makeup.

In 1967, there was only one black stuntman in Hollywood. Then a group of African Americans formed the Black Stuntmen's Association. Harris got his big break in 1971 with the movie *Dirty Harry*. In the film, Clint Eastwood shoots him, and Harris has to fall down concrete steps.

But things still weren't easy. White stuntmen didn't want to share their skills with African Americans. Black stuntmen couldn't join the training schools. So Harris and other African Americans taught themselves.

As one of the first black stuntmen, Harris helped open doors for others in movies. In the late 1960s, there were no African Americans working

Harris at the bottom of the concrete steps in his famous action scene from *Dirty Harry*.

in wardrobe or makeup. They weren't operating cameras. There was one black movie producer. Harris and the Black Stuntmen's Association helped change Hollywood.

THINK ABOUT IT

Harris and the other stuntmen taught themselves how to perform safely. What is something you taught yourself to do? Would it have been easier if someone had shown you?

2016

Year the National Museum of African American History and Culture opened

- This Smithsonian museum is in Washington, DC.
- Its collections include props and photos from the Black Stuntmen's Association.
- Two caps and a shirt worn by Willie Harris are on display.

15

Lillian Leitzel: Spinning Under the Big Top

Lillian Leitzel was born in Germany in 1891. Her mother was a trapeze artist. Lillian wanted to be just like her mother. She worked hard to learn the skills. At 14 years old, she joined her mother's aerial troupe. Known as the Leamy Sisters, they performed all around the world.

Leitzel's solo act began with the Roman rings. Two ropes with silver rings on the ends hung from the ceiling of the circus tent. Often, they were 50 or 60 feet (15 or 18 m) in the air. There was no net below. Leitzel climbed up a rope to reach the rings. For six minutes, she gave the crowd a graceful acrobatic performance.

In 1911, Leitzel introduced a new stunt that would become the second part of her act. Near the top of the tent, she grabbed onto a single rope. She slipped her hand

through a loop and hung by her wrist. Then she threw her body over her shoulders and started rotating. With each turn, her arm dislocated from her shoulder. The crowd would count the rotations. She usually performed more than 100 rotations each time.

Lillian Leitzel in 1931.

One time, she completed 239 rotations.

In 1915, Leitzel joined Ringling Brothers Circus. She quickly became the star. The crowds loved her. Reporters wrote about her act in newspapers and magazines. She became so famous that the name Leitzel was a household word.

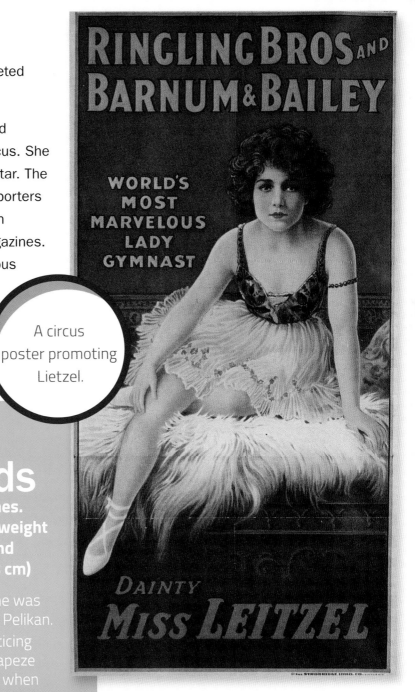

A circus poster promoting Lietzel.

95 pounds

**4 feet 9 inches.
Lillian Leitzel's weight
(43.1 kg) and
height (144.8 cm)**

- Leitzel's real name was Leopoldina Alitza Pelikan.
- She started practicing on a miniature trapeze and Roman rings when she was three or four years old.
- She died from a fall in 1931.

Kitty O'Neil: Record-Setting Wonder Woman

Kitty O'Neil was born in Texas in 1946. She was part white and part Native American. When O'Neil was a baby, a high fever caused her to lose her hearing. But her mother pushed her to live a normal life. O'Neil learned to play the piano and the cello, as well as different sports. She learned to read lips.

Kitty O'Neil in 1976.

During the 1970s, O'Neil worked as a stunt double for movie stars. She was actress Lynda Carter's stunt double in the hit TV series *Wonder Woman*. For one stunt, O'Neil jumped 127 feet (39 m) from the roof of a hotel. She later broke that record by jumping 180 feet (55 m) from a helicopter.

O'Neil broke many other records. She set world records for speed in a jet-powered boat and on water skis. In December 1976, she went to the Alvord Desert in Oregon. The desert is a dried lake bed. She wanted to beat the women's land speed record of 321 miles per hour (517 km/hr).

1

Number of bones Kitty O'Neil broke during her lifetime

- O'Neil was 5 feet 2 inches tall (157.5 cm) and weighed just 97 pounds (44 kg).
- Her small stature helped her withstand the strong forces of acceleration.
- She believed her deafness helped her stay focused.

O'Neil performing a stunt for the TV show *Wonder Woman* in 1979.

She made two runs in a three-wheeled rocket car. The average of both runs was 512.71 miles per hour (825.13 km/hr). She smashed the old record. O'Neil was the fastest woman in the world.

FOR MEN ONLY

During one of her runs in Oregon, O'Neil reached 618 miles per hour (994.6 km/hr). She wanted to try again. She thought she could break the men's record of 630.388 miles per hour (1,014.5 km/hr). She also wanted to break the sound barrier. But the opportunity was given to a male driver.

Harry Houdini: Hanging Out Over the Streets

Harry Houdini was born in 1874 in Budapest, Hungary. When he was four years old, he moved with his family to Wisconsin. They moved again when he was 13, this time to New York City. While there, Harry began his career as a magician. He was about 20 years old. But the crowds didn't come to see his

42

Houdini's age when he performed the straitjacket stunt in Pittsburgh

- Houdini's real name was Ehrich Weiss.
- Because of his skill, he was called the Handcuff King.
- He died in 1926 from a ruptured appendix.

magic. Instead, he drew them with his daring escapes.

By 1895, Houdini was using handcuffs in his acts. During his performances, he escaped from straitjackets, jails, and boxes. Sometimes he was chained up underwater. By 1899, Houdini was performing all over Europe and the United States.

To bring people in to see his shows, Houdini often did a stunt outdoors in the

Harry Houdini performs one of his manacled jumps into Boston's Charles River in 1908.

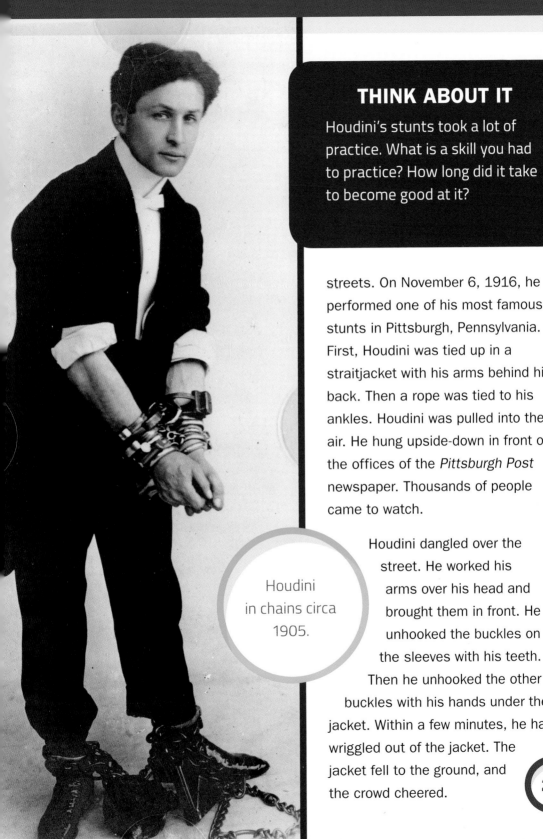

Houdini
in chains circa
1905.

THINK ABOUT IT

Houdini's stunts took a lot of practice. What is a skill you had to practice? How long did it take to become good at it?

streets. On November 6, 1916, he performed one of his most famous stunts in Pittsburgh, Pennsylvania. First, Houdini was tied up in a straitjacket with his arms behind his back. Then a rope was tied to his ankles. Houdini was pulled into the air. He hung upside-down in front of the offices of the *Pittsburgh Post* newspaper. Thousands of people came to watch.

Houdini dangled over the street. He worked his arms over his head and brought them in front. He unhooked the buckles on the sleeves with his teeth. Then he unhooked the other buckles with his hands under the jacket. Within a few minutes, he had wriggled out of the jacket. The jacket fell to the ground, and the crowd cheered.

21

Janeshia Adams-Ginyard: Paving the Way with a Spear

Janeshia Adams-Ginyard was born in Los Angeles, California, on Valentine's Day 1984. She started running track when she was eight years old. She continued with sports throughout high school and college. She ran track and played volleyball.

She was a member of the US National Bobsled team.

One day, she watched a movie with a man running. Since she had run track, she believed she could do that, too. The stunt people were listed at the end of the movie.

Janeshia Adams-Ginyard arrives at the *Black Panther* world premier in Hollywood, CA, in 2018.

18
Weeks Adams-Ginyard spent filming *Black Panther*

- Adams-Ginyard also worked as a professional wrestler named Frost.
- In her first seven years of acting, she performed in 25 different movies and TV shows.
- She stunt-doubled in Avengers: *Infinity War* and *Godzilla: King of the Monsters*.

Black Panther is a superhero film based on the Marvel Comics character.

GOODBYE, HAIR

The stunts were not the only difficult part of *Black Panther*. When Adams-Ginyard got the role, she had long hair. But the character is bald. Adams-Ginyard would have to shave her head. At first, she cried. She almost didn't accept the role. Her friends convinced her it was worth it.

Adams-Ginyard decided she could be one.

Adams-Ginyard started doing stunts in 2010. She spent the first few years just training. She learned gymnastics and martial arts. At the same time, she took jobs as extras in films. There are not many African American stuntwomen. She told people she was willing to do stunts. Finally, she was offered her first stunt job.

Adams-Ginyard's hard work paid off. In 2016, she tried out for the movie *Black Panther*. She got a role as

part of the all-female special forces. She was also the stunt double for actress Danai Gurira. Adams-Ginyard trained with a bo staff for eight hours a day. On the set, she had to use a real spear. She helped pave the way for African American female daredevils.

Debbie Lawler: An Angel on a Motorcycle

Debbie Lawler was born in Oregon in 1952. Her father was a motorcycle racer. She received her own motorcycle for her 12th birthday. Two

$50,000
What Lawler earned from her record-breaking jump at the Astrodome

- A month later, Knievel jumped over 17 trucks.
- Even though Knievel beat her record, Lawler was a sensation with the public.
- The Kenner toy company created the Debbie Lawler Daredevil Jump Set for girls.

years later, she started racing. As she got older, Lawler worked as a professional model. But she wanted to be the first woman to jump a motorcycle, ramp to ramp. At that time, there were no women jumping motorcycles.

Lawler began jumping professionally in 1972. She wore a light blue leather outfit with pink hearts on it. She jumped her motorcycle at fairs and speedways across the country. In March 1973, Lawler jumped a total of 76 feet (23 m) over a line of parked cars. She set a world record for distance in women's motorcycle jumping.

At the time, other daredevils were also jumping motorcycles. The most famous was a stuntman named Evel Knievel. He was known for his motorcycle jumps over buses and cars. Fans called Lawler the Female Evel Knievel and the Flying Angel.

Knievel held a record of jumping 15 parked trucks indoors. Lawler wanted to beat that record. On February 3, 1974, she went to the National Championship Indoor Motorcycle Race at the Houston Astrodome in Texas. She was going to try to jump over 16 Chevy pickup trucks. She was 21 years old. A mistake would injure or even kill her. But she made the 101-foot (30.8 m) jump and earned a spot in the *Guinness Book of World Records*.

Lawler making her world record jump in 1973.

Alain Robert: A Real-Life Spider Man

Alain Robert was born in France in 1962. When he was small, he was afraid of heights. But when he was 11 years old, he was locked out of his apartment. He had to climb seven floors up the building to get in. As a teenager, Robert became an accomplished mountain and rock climber.

When Robert was 19, he fell from a cliff. Doctors told him he would never climb again. He wouldn't accept that. At about 30 years old, he started climbing tall buildings. Most of the time, he doesn't use any safety equipment. Known as the Human Spider, he has climbed buildings around the world.

In October 2018, Robert decided to climb a building in London, England. He chose the Heron Tower. The skyscraper is one of the tallest buildings in the city. It is 755 feet (230 m) tall.

On October 25, Robert started to scale the building. He didn't have any ropes or other equipment. Many people came to watch. Police had to stop traffic and move the crowd out of the road. Fire trucks and an ambulance came in case he fell. But Robert made it to the top in approximately 50 minutes.

26

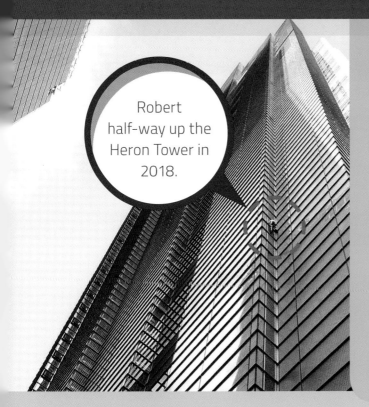

Robert half-way up the Heron Tower in 2018.

46
Number of floors in the Heron Tower

- Robert used chalk to create friction between his skin and the building.
- He taped his fingers and wore thin gloves so his hands wouldn't get cut up.
- Robert's family was confident he'd make it to the top.

AN ILLEGAL ACTIVITY

Sometimes Robert gets permission to climb a building. But he didn't have permission to climb the Heron Tower. When he reached the top, he was arrested. He has been arrested more than 100 times for trespassing. This time, police said he caused a public nuisance. However, the people still enjoyed watching him.

More Impossible Daredevil Stunts

Flight of the Flat Earther

"Mad" Mike Hughes believes the earth is flat. He wanted to see if it was true. So in 2018, he built a rocket and sent himself up. He soared almost 2,000 feet (609.6 m) into the air before the rocket came down again. Hughes made a hard landing, but he was all right.

Highest Free Fall

Felix Baumgartner is a skydiver from Austria. In 2012, he jumped out of a balloon 128,100 feet (39 km) in the air. He set a new record for the highest free fall. During the fall, he reached a speed of 833.9 miles per hour (1,342 km/h). He landed safely with a parachute.

Capsule that was attached to a balloon that Baumgartner jumped from in 2012.

First Stuntwoman

Helen Gibson was the first professional American stuntwoman. She trained as a trick rider on horses. In 1914, she began doubling for an actress names Helen Holmes. In one scene, she had to jump from a speeding motorcycle onto a fast-moving train.

Riding Bareback

May Wirth was an Australian circus performer. One stunt in 1916 involved two galloping horses. Standing on the back of the first horse, she did a somersault into the air. She landed on the back of the second horse that was galloping behind.

Mary Wirth in 1920.

29

Glossary

aerial
Something that happens in the air.

air currents
Air moving from an area of high pressure to an area of lower pressure.

bo staff
A long piece of wood used as a weapon.

boarding school
A school where the students live as well as learn.

bobsled
A sled with a crew of two or four people used to race down a steep ice-covered track.

discrimination
The unfair treatment of people because of their race.

dislocate
To move the top of the arm bone out of the shoulder socket.

martial arts
Skills that originated as forms of self-defense or attack, including karate and judo.

segregated
Separated because of race.

straitjacket
A strong piece of special clothing that uses buckles, straps, and long sleeves that can be tied together to restrain people who might hurt themselves or others.

tandem
To be attached to an instructor with a harness

wingsuit
A one-piece suit that allows a person to glide through the air when freefalling.

Read More

Monnig, Alex. *Stunt Performers in Action.* Dangerous Jobs in Action. Mankato, MN: The Child's World, 2017.

Omoth, Tyler. *Stunning Motorcycle Stunts.* Edge Books: Wild Stunts. Mankato, MN: Capstone Publishing, 2016.

Skeers, Linda. *Women Who Dared: 52 Fearless Daredevils, Adventurers & Rebels.* Naperville, IL: Sourcebooks Inc., 2017.

Tougas, Joe. *Mind-Blowing Movie Stunts.* Edge Books: Wild Stunts. Mankato, MN: Capstone Publishing, 2016.

Visit 12StoryLibrary.com

Scan the code or use your school's login at **12StoryLibrary.com** for recent updates about this topic and a full digital version of this book. Enjoy free access to:

- Digital ebook
- Breaking news updates
- Live content feeds
- Videos, interactive maps, and graphics
- Additional web resources

Note to educators: Visit 12StoryLibrary.com/register to sign up for free premium website access. Enjoy live content plus a full digital version of every 12-Story Library book you own for every student at your school.

Index

About the Author

Samantha S. Bell lives in upstate
South Carolina with her family and lots
of animals. She is the author of more
than 100 nonfiction books for children.